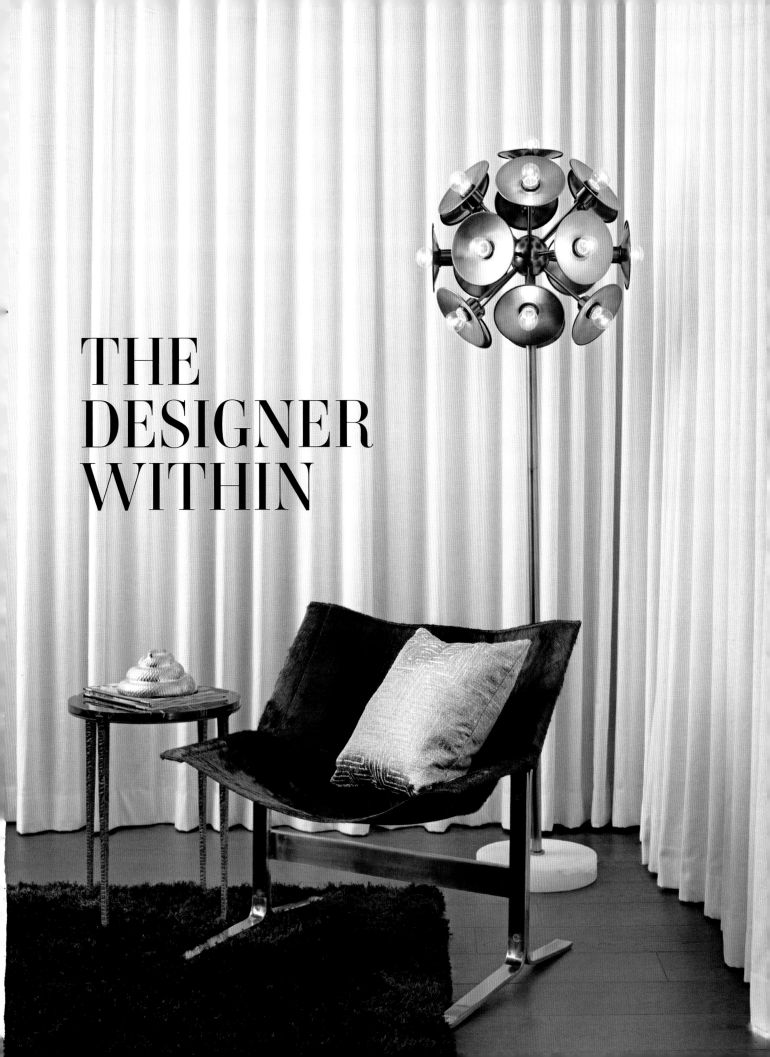

THE
DESIGNER
WITHIN

THE DESIGNER WITHIN

A PROFESSIONAL GUIDE
TO A WELL-STYLED HOME

John McClain

Principal Photographer ZEKE RUELAS

GIBBS SMITH
TO ENRICH AND INSPIRE HUMANKIND

I dedicate this book to a man who could not read or write but taught me so much more than any textbook ever could. To my grandfather, Vernon Bearden, thank you for your guidance, knowledge, and unconditional love. I promise to continue spreading your wisdom and sharing your lessons to the best of my ability.

CONTENTS

FOREWORD

By Loren Ruch
Group SVP, Development & Production, HGTV

Sometimes life introduces you to people you just need to know. On a chance meeting in Key West, Florida, John McClain came into my life fifteen years ago with his smiling face and gregarious personality. It was obvious from the start that John's true passion and talent was interior design. He would come alive whenever he spoke of design, telling stories about creating furniture and décor as a child and space planning his family's homes to better suit their lifestyle. He was designing for function and fashion even as a kid! Our friendship continued to grow, and our professional paths crossed when he was independently cast on HGTV's *First Time Design* where he was a true natural, lighting up the screen. It was the perfect entry into an amazing career creating beautiful spaces, and I'm so proud to say I've gotten to watch him live out his dreams from the very beginning. The world has a master plan in place even when you don't see it for yourself—it brought into my life someone incredibly passionate, fiercely talented, insanely fun to work with, and a dear friend—symmetry at its finest. This beautiful book, *The Designer Within*, perfectly embodies John's amazing design skills as well as his genuine passion to share all that he has learned with his readers. Personally, it's a reflection of everything I could have ever wished for a smiling stranger grabbing a pina colada poolside next to me fifteen years ago.

INTRODUCTION

There has always been a designer within me. As a child, I could see the potential for beauty in almost everything and had an eye for arranging things in artful ways. I don't even think I knew why I was drawn to the allure of the home, but I was. From a young age, my mother took me to yard sales and thrift stores, where we would find the best antiques in the worst condition, buy them for nearly nothing, and take them home to sand, stain, and seal them until they gleamed in perfect antiquity. I didn't know it at the time, but this was my calling. My family had a big influence on my career path; they were always building or designing something—from homes to barns to furniture, you name it—and I was enamored by it all! To think that something that started as a mere idea could turn into an entire home was so intriguing to an eight-year-old's inquisitive brain. I began to look inside myself and realized that I too held the same method of thinking as my imaginative family members, with my own ideas and designs floating around my creative brain space. But what to do with those ideas?

When I was sixteen, I made the decision to design and build my own "retreat" in an unused, unbuilt room adjacent to our family garage. When I say unbuilt, I mean that it was wall studs and a roof only. I called my grandfather and asked if he would help me. He immediately said yes. So, he and I spent the entire summer designing, building, and ultimately finishing my bedroom suite, complete with a full-size bathroom and a walk-in closet! I found an antique claw-foot tub at a house that was being torn down and refurbished it, bought discounted plumbing fixtures and lights, and painted a rolling cloud mural on my bathroom ceiling to construct this special escape for myself. I used every bit of money I had saved from my after-school and summer jobs and created a place that I truly loved—and my grandfather and I did it all with our own hands. The rewards were plentiful both visually and psychologically.

I felt a sense of pride, honor, and complete joy in seeing that transformation. Even though I didn't have the funds needed to create an entirely new space, I didn't limit myself and instead used creativity and ingenuity to achieve my goal. The final product literally had my blood, sweat, and tears in it. I soon found I was limited only by how I limit myself. A few years later, I purchased my first home at age twenty-one—resulting in the full renovation of an 1880s farmhouse—and at that point I knew there was no turning back. Design was in me, and I was in design.

My family may not have been wealthy, but we were resourceful. Since we didn't have the means to buy or build whatever we wanted, we had to constantly think outside the box and develop creative ways to bring our designs to life. This taught me an invaluable lesson: no matter the financial status, everyone deserves a beautiful place to call home. Today, I hold these lessons close to my heart, and I mindfully apply them to my firm's designs, whether I'm designing a multimillion-dollar home or a starter house for a new family. The love and

appreciation for a place to call home is the same, regardless of the size or value. Honestly, my clients' reactions mean more to me than a big paycheck. I have had clients cry, dance, and even stand speechless after seeing their home's completion. The power of home is real, and I'm so blessed to be able to have a part in creating that for so many deserving families. I sincerely want every person on the planet to walk into a home that hugs them. What do I mean by that? Your home is that one special, unrivaled sanctuary that should greet you like a warm hug every time you walk through the door.

My life changed for the better when I realized design was my future, and I knew the designer within me was clawing to get out. And guess what? You have a designer within you too! It may not be as obvious as it was for me, but I promise they are in there! It is that part of you that awakens when you see a gorgeous chair or a sparkling chandelier. It's the thirst to have pieces in your home that feel special and unique. And it's the love for your family and for yourself that fuels your desire to make your living spaces as personalized and as beautiful as you deserve.

Over the past thirteen years, my career as an interior-design professional has afforded me the opportunities to work on and in some of the most beautiful homes and with some of the most beautiful people—inside and out. Within these projects, I have also honed a design process that has yielded proven results. From the initial design conception to the final vase being placed on the shelf, the systems and design processes I have in place always lead to happy clients and a happy designer.

Now I'm pulling back that proverbial curtain to reveal design solutions for your own spaces. Make no mistake, this book is not about cutting corners or designing for less; it is about truly diving into your soul and exposing all your design wants and wishes. It is about understanding those key components that lead to a successful design. And mostly, it is about exploring your creative side, the side you may not yet even know is there.

My goal with this book is to help bring the designer within you to the surface. This doesn't mean that you must do a full renovation, but it does mean that I invite you to ask yourself, "What would make me the happiest when I walk into my home?" Could it be a better room or furniture layout or a bolder color palette? Or is it simply the need for a new area rug that has you stumped? Throughout this book, I guide you to unlocking the space that holds your home's potential. Moreover, I share my own process when it comes to creating the elegant designs on these pages. There will be lots of "aha" moments for you as I dissect a selection of my favorite projects and reveal the specific reasons why these designs were a success. I also share tips from my own experience that will help you avoid failures and potential disasters. You'll find answers to the most-asked design questions that I receive as we peruse some truly beautiful images of homes that fill me with pride. In addition to being elegant and beautiful, my designs tend to be practical; I don't like a home that is too precious or that feels like a museum of untouchables rather than a cozy home that nurtures the needs of those inside its walls. I design homes to be lived in—alluring, functional, and, most importantly, happy homes—and you're about to learn how I do it.

Grab your key and open the front door. You're about to find the designer within *you!*

THE DESIGN PROCESS

Design projects demand detailed processes that lead to success. Here are the basic steps I follow to start and complete every project.

STEP 1: DEFINE YOUR NEEDS AND DESIRES

When deciding to begin any design plan—for myself or for a client—I always start with what is really desired and needed. I ask my clients to dive deep explore what truly matters to them in design. Let's start with color: what colors make you happy, relaxed, excited, or even hungry? Aesthetic: what vibe would you like to evoke in your home? Is it vibrant glam? Modern with clean lines? Or maybe it's a light, all-neutral, transitional space to relax in after a long day. Travel: what past vacation destination or even hotel stay really stands out in your mind and why? No matter the design goal, you will only achieve it if you allow yourself to *feel* the design and recognize what you want it to accomplish. Identify the ultimate goal you are trying to achieve. Is function paramount in your ideal space? Or do you focus on the colors, textures, and materials in your dream room? Maybe it's both (hint: it should be both). Are you envisioning a kitchen that will hold all of your favorite cooking supplies while still being design forward? Just know, you can have it all, at least during this first design planning session.

Write down all of the things you're picturing. I like to use bullet points to separate my thoughts. Use descriptive words or specific examples of what you are envisioning as your ideal space. Your words do not need to be organized in any particular way. This is your brainstorming session, and there are zero judgments on your clerical skills.

STEP 2:
FIND YOUR INSPIRATION

Now that you have your list of wants and needs, it's time to start organizing them. I am mindful that most projects have strict budgets, but for this first critical exercise, let's pretend money is no object. Build on the foundation of Step 1 by finding precise examples of your dream kitchen, bedroom, bath, or any other room. Start by tearing inspirational images from magazine pages or by starting a Pinterest or Houzz board and digitally saving your finds there. However, don't limit yourself to images of entire rooms or homes. If it's just one sofa (and by the way, it is a sofa not a couch), or a lamp, or even something as simple as a doorknob, save it! These will become the foundation of your design plan. Once you have found what inspires you, organize those images by room or space. This will help to further develop each part of your new home or room. As you are saving these images, ask yourself, "Why do I like this?" Then make a note of what you like on the actual page or in the notes section of the online platform you are using. You will soon start to see a pattern developing for your selections.

STEP 3:
CREATE YOUR PROJECT DIRECTION BOARD

You've taken the first step and gathered inspirational images that grab your attention, so let's create what I call a "project direction board." This step is simply the assemblage of your finds in Step 2. Rather than showing the exact items you'll use, the project direction board will act as a mood board, capturing how the project should feel. Compile the research that you have collected thus far into one or two presentations per space. Don't worry about how you assemble these together; we just want to be able to review the images as a grouping: pinned physically to a foam core board or "pinned" electronically together in a software program to get a true feel for each room's design direction.

STEP 4:
GET SPECIFIC

Utilizing your project direction board, it's time to begin making *specific* selections for your home. You will need full measurements of your rooms, including sizes of windows and doors, as well as the full list of items you want to incorporate. I recommend initially sourcing two to three options for each type of item so you can compare your selections and make the right choice (or so you can simply reselect if your first choice is unavailable). Decide on a total budget for each space as well as a budget for each individual product. Do some online research on low, medium, and high priced items in each category to better understand the quality and construction of each piece as it corresponds to price.

Next, you'll be adding your options to final boards, one board per room or space: your design boards. The design boards can once again be physical or digital. I prefer a physical design board so that I can touch the fabrics and finishes while seeing the printed images of the sofa, chair, or lighting that will be in each space. For a physical board, print or cut out each image of your products, and then pin or glue fabrics, metals, fringe, paint swatches, etc., to a large foam core board. Pinning makes it easy to move things around later should you change your mind about something. (T-pins are my go-to for easy pinning). After you have all of the options in front of you, narrow them down to your favorite item per category. One sofa, one chair, one chandelier, and so on; be decisive on your choices while considering how each component coordinates with the group. At the end of Step 4, you should have a design board with specific choices for every area you are designing. I recommend starting a spreadsheet as well, including each room, item, vendor, color, finish, dimensions, and price. This will help you keep track as you order all of your design pieces. Be proud of your accomplishment and start ordering your products, because your design is ready to be born!

STEP 5:
ACCESSORIZE

Congratulations, the hard part is over! You have worked your way through the design process, narrowed down your options, and acquired and placed your items in their respective spaces. It's time to add the final touches to your design plan—the jewelry of the room: accessories! Never underestimate the power of good accessorizing. It's what makes the rooms you see online and in magazines feel truly complete. Accessories include any object that will reside on flat surfaces—such as tables, bookcases, fireplace mantels, or shelves—but also art, plants, mirrors, and bar accessories (musts in my house).

You will want to establish a separate accessory budget for each room, but first you will take inventory of your current accessories. Clear off a large table and assemble all the accessories you currently own. Look them over closely and ask yourself, "What is a must-have that I simply cannot live without?" These can be family heirloom items, trinkets from travels, your favorite books, etc. Place these must-keep items in a separate area. Now go back to your design board, or, better yet, simply walk into the spaces and choose items from your collection that will best accessorize each room. You should consider colors, textures, metallics, scale (varying sizes), and amount needed when reviewing each room. For instance, if you have a large bookshelf, you know you will need, at minimum, lots of books. I like to group books together by the color of their bindings and assemble them on shelves accordingly.

As you are assembling your favorite accessories, start a donation box. This box is for accessories that are in poor condition, dated, or simply the wrong style or color for your newly designed home.

Next, develop a budget of what you would like to spend on new accessories per space. Perhaps you have almost all that you need for accessorizing your family room but are still missing a few items. You could allocate a small amount of the budget to complete your accessory list for this room. However, if your entry hall has some empty console tables, bookshelves, or lots of walls, you will need to consider a higher budget to properly accessorize this room.

STEP 6:
HAVE FUN

It goes without saying that interior design can be taxing, just like any other task, but if you know that the benefit will far outweigh the work involved, why not have fun along the way? I always say "trust the process," and with this book and these steps, I hope that you can find joy in design, even in the most challenging times.

Admittedly, there will be times when you want to throw in the towel and forget about the entire thing. When this happens, ask yourself what made you feel this way, write it down, and never let it happen again. The process you see here is tried and true. I have used it hundreds of times for my clients and for myself, so trust that it will also work for you. When those difficulties occur, pull out your project design board and reflect on what is to come. Touch the fabrics, lovingly stare at the product images, and see yourself in the future space, using and loving it. Your new home design is just around the corner, so set your eye on the prize and keep moving. We are in this together.

" When painting a room a dark color, consider using a higher sheen paint to add reflectivity to the surfaces. This allows light to bounce off the darker color, making it feel less heavy. "

LISTEN TO
YOUR HEART

There's no place like home . . . Isn't that the truth? No place has that "kick off your shoes, make dinner, and hang with your loved ones" kind of feeling quite like the place you call home. So why wouldn't we want to nurture this special place that takes such good care of us?

One of my first questions for any client is "what does the word *home* mean to you?" The answer is always some combination of peace, comfort, style, and overall happiness. The key to a good design is including aspects of all those feelings. Also key: listening to your own heart, not your neighbor, not the popular TV show, and definitely not the catalog you just received in the mail. These areas of inspiration are fleeting; they tend to be filled with trendy, non-original designs. Trust your instincts! This sounds easy, but it requires you to identify what would bring you the most happiness in your home and take risks to make it happen. This step is difficult for most because if you haven't seen a certain design before, can it—or should it—be done? I can tell you this: every design idea that has become well-liked started with one person who took a risk and decided that the design could, and should, be developed.

The project featured here is my own home. I will admit, it's much easier for me to take risks in my own spaces than in some of my clients' homes. I want you to see my creative processes when it comes to design decisions, but I also want to help you realize that your only limitation is your mindset.

For my home, I wanted to be bold while still maintaining a timeless aesthetic. I wanted to go all in with my design, bringing in all the color, pattern, and out-of-the-box thinking that can sometimes be a little intimidating. Mostly, I wanted the design to be personal to my husband, Peter, and me and for it to truly represent us.

Another lesson learned: just because something is brand new doesn't mean it's right for you and your aesthetic. My home was brand-new construction, but it wasn't design forward and didn't have any of the quality custom features that are important to me. So, I gutted a brand-new house and started over. I know not everyone can (or should) do this, but while you might like some of the things about your house, don't force yourself to like them all or to live with them just because they are new or "good enough." Here, then, is my heart-filled, no-holds-barred ode to design, my own home, lovingly named "Modern Loft Bungalow."

Previous overleaf: The entry of my home sets the tone for everything you are about to see. Walls, ceilings, doors, and trim are swathed in a rich burgundy paint. Stair risers and railings are painted black to allow only the slightest differentiation in color. I love a gallery wall done well, and this one starts at the bottom of the staircase and leads your eye to the second floor.

Above: A mirror in the entry serves two great purposes: a decorative feature to expand the size of a small space and a spot for a first or last look before opening the door.

Opposite: The view from the loft showcases the full drama of my home's fireplace. The sheer size of the installation is a focal point as well as a bridge between the living room and the loft.

Overleaf: The open-floor-plan living room has a small dining area to separate the kitchen from the living area. The living room's grand feature is the twenty-foot-high ceiling, further amplified by a custom, two-story fireplace. Dynamic dining room art by Tony Curry enlivens that space.

Opposite: The massive fireplace design is further enhanced by the chic, industrial, multi-tier pendant light. Notice the television is recessed into the fireplace to create a smooth and seamless front façade.

Above: The fireplace is the crowning jewel of the living room. Made of porcelain slabs and leather, the design is an homage to midcentury and art deco styles. The fireplace uses lighted water vapor, and I added selenite logs to create a truly unique fireplace experience.

> " Properly styling a coffee table is much like styling a book-shelf. Must-haves include books with some sort of "book topper," such as a brass object or any small accent piece, one to two objects with height, and one bowl or round object. "

Previous overleaf: Looking back from the living room into the kitchen and up to the loft, you see the importance of continuity in design. Notice in the kitchen how multiple smaller decorative lights were used instead of the standard recessed lighting. Bold art zones the dining area.

Opposite: A play on lines, a custom, patent-leather mirror and a ribbed bar cabinet separate the kitchen from the powder bath. I love a dedicated space to mix drinks, and this area is accessible from anywhere in the main living area.

Overleaf: A complete renovation, the new kitchen is simultaneously classic and contemporary. From this vantage point, you see my take on the waterfall edge, with an angular countertop layered on a brass backing. The raised portion of the peninsula bar features a contrasting quartz material, which gives a bit of privacy to the kitchen counters and also holds a rear electrical outlet.

"Add one piece of interesting dissonance to every room. It should be a piece that feels slightly out of place and makes everyone stop and take notice. "

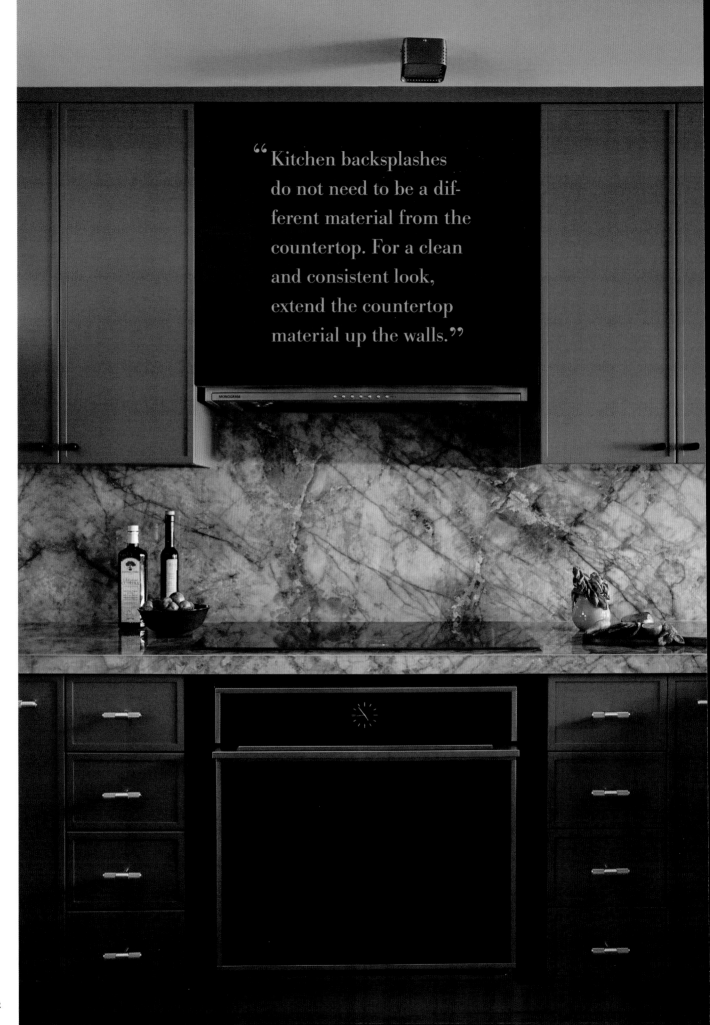

"Kitchen backsplashes do not need to be a different material from the countertop. For a clean and consistent look, extend the countertop material up the walls."

Opposite: The cooking center showcases an induction cooktop and a wall oven. The wall oven is installed below the counter, and I added dark-colored side panels to visually pair the width of the oven with the cooktop. The ventilation hood is hidden under a faux-metal cabinetry door.

Above left: The brass accents continue with a modern kitchen faucet presiding over a gray composite sink. Though this kitchen counter-top looks like real marble, it's actually durable and functional porcelain slabs.

Above right: From inside the kitchen, you see the visual connection to the living area. Though these look like regular drawers, the cabinetry panels are actually hiding two refrigeration drawers.

Right: The mixing of materials is what makes this kitchen look and feel custom. Charcoal-stained wood veneer clads two adjoining walls that house the full-size refrigerator. The right wall of gray cabinetry holds a five-in-one oven, including microwave. Sexy, textured, oversized brass pulls blend the larger refrigerator wall with the gray cabinetry.

Previous overleaf: A voluminous room needs oversized furniture, and this custom sofa fits the bill. Modular pieces form the full sofa, where its clean lines are softened by the pleating detail on the sides, back, and front. The oversized palm tree draws the eye upward to the loft staircase.

Above: I love a great coffee tablescape. This one mixes flowers, books, and fruit.

Opposite: This is a multilevel home, which means several staircases and landings. The impactful art by Elena Carlie punctuates the long hallway while inviting you to keep exploring. Floor-to-ceiling door panels were installed to conceal what was formerly several individual doors in this passageway.

" The mix of small, medium, and large patterns in addition to some areas of solid color is key to making patterns play well together in a space. "

Previous overleaf: The final floor of this multilevel home is the most vibrant room yet. Designed as an ode to the lounges of yesteryear, this cozy space is pattern play at its pinnacle, and its warm color palette lures you in. Commissioned artwork by Shawni Young features one of my favorite people and the perfect host for this loft party, Dolly Parton.

Opposite: Wall-to-wall drapery almost feels like wallpaper when it covers the entire back wall, while also concealing a sliding patio door. A pocket niche was created beside the end cabinetry to hold the drapery.

Above: Nothing says lounge like a Chesterfield sofa, and the back of the piece is as beautiful as the front.

" If your furniture piece can be seen from multiple angles, be sure both the front and back are pleasing to the eye. "

Opposite: In order to fully function as an entertaining lounge, a television was a must. Metallic wallpaper wakes up the otherwise visually quiet niche.

Above right: I loved this pendant light from the minute I saw it. The midcentury styling is modernized by casting the LED light up from the socket below.

Right: Though this looks like simple cabinetry, it actually houses a refrigerator and ice maker for entertaining made easy. Side cabinets run floor to ceiling, giving lots of valuable storage.

"Instead of replacing your bathroom cabinet, consider painting it and changing out the door hardware. This simple revision can result in the look of a brand-new piece."

Opposite: I simply must have a powerful powder room! Rich, deep colors draw you into this small room, where heavily patterned wallpaper is balanced by a geometric, embossed tile. The blue-and-brass sink vanity allows the eye to rest amid the color and pattern explosion.

Above: Black, white, and brown shades are extended into the bathroom adjoining the guest bedroom. Black-and-white floor tiles bring some much-needed pattern to this neutral palette.

Opposite and above left: A lovely vignette encapsulates my favorite components of this bedroom: texture, color, and scale. The wallpaper is made of mica, and the bed is upholstered in durable and beautiful vinyl. The sphere pendants are a nice juxtaposition to the prismatic wallpaper.

Above right: Drawing on my travel inspiration, the main bathroom was completely renovated with a nod to the design of Harrods Food Halls in London. Luxe, intricately patterned marble, oversized turned legs, and black cabinetry feel vintage and simultaneously current.

Right: The mirror over each vanity was inlaid into the tile with a vintage brass finish frame added. Notice how the brass tones carry up from the vanity legs to the plumbing fixtures and then to the lights and mirror. Verticality was emphasized by elongated lighting, tall mirrors, and cabinetry that touches the ceilings.

Opposite: The main bath shower is pattern galore with marble tiles on the floor, wall, and ceiling. Each tile was specifically placed during installation to create an even more detailed result. The rainfall showerhead combines lights, water, and even sound.

Above: The bathroom connects to the home office and continues the color palette from the associated space. The custom, dark-stained vanity is capped by a distinctive quartz countertop. Chrome light fixture, hardware, and plumbing fixtures add just the right amount of glamour.

Left: The home office is simple and functional but with some elegant additions. The desk is made of three filing cabinets with a beautiful porcelain slab cut for the desktop. Wallpaper can be used in places other than on walls, and here the ceiling is covered in a textural brass-colored wallcovering, which highlights an oversized, round, brass pendant.

Overleaf left: The guest room is mucho multifunctional. A beautiful wood, rattan, and brass desk floats in the center of the room, anchored by a zebra-print rug and a black, faceted credenza of my own design. The sofa bed is chic for sitting and functional for sleeping.

Overleaf right: The neutral color palette in this room was intended to give the eye a rest from the color filling the rest of the home. A funky and fun handmade side table is the perfect accompaniment to the Hollywood Regency sofa and the midcentury-patterned drapery.

IT'S ALL IN THE MIX

The mix of design styles is critical to a room's design. Design today (and forever more, if you ask me) is an interesting blend of several different design genres but with commonalities that bond them together. Please know that not only are you allowed to mix design styles, but you also most definitely *should* mix styles and periods.

The key to making the mix work is to consider color, shape, and scale. These are the very same things you consider for every room you will design, but they are even more important in a room of mixed styles. Find commonalities among elements, such as the same color, the same metal accent finish, or similar shapes. My favorite design periods to mix are midcentury, art deco, and contemporary. There are always commonalities among these styles that will allow them to play in the same design sandbox.

HOLY CHIC

I genuinely appreciate and celebrate all design genres, from midcentury to modern, traditional to contemporary, and beyond. Unapologetically, all these design styles meld to make the John McClain Design signature look. Many designers tend to limit themselves to a specific type of design, and they stay strictly and specifically within that category, which is totally fine—for them. However, I genuinely find the beauty and appeal in all types of design, and I particularly love it when adventurous clients knock on our door to ask us to create something truly unique and special for them. On top of juxtaposing different styles, you will hopefully also notice that every project that I design has an underlying tone of elegance; my favorite vehicle to properly showcase elegance is through chic design.

I adore the word *chic*. Chic brings to mind a perfectly tailored Chanel suit or Jackie Kennedy Onassis on a yacht. Or even better, Jackie Kennedy Onassis wearing Chanel on a yacht. Well, you get the picture. Chic is a blend of luxury, sophistication, and carefully considered elements, whether in fashion or home design. But a home must be a living, breathing, and, most importantly, a useful space, so you might be wondering, "Can you logically and effectively combine 'comfort' and 'chic'? The two words are not, and *should not*, be mutually exclusive. You can have a home that feels tailored and luxurious while also having a home where you can enjoy a pizza dinner on the coffee table. I mentioned Jackie O on her yacht earlier, but what about the iconic image of Jackie riding an elephant? This image probably better illustrates the mix of practicality and sophistication. Your home can operate much in the same way as the dichotomy of Jackie in her elegant yellow dress on the back of a large jungle animal. Still not sure? Stick with me and I'll show you how.

In this chapter, you will see images that exude comfortable chic. The two homes here are designed around elegance but are both also used by busy families. Again, the terms *chic and comfortable* can live in harmony together, but now I'm going to throw in the not-so-sexy word durable. Do I even dare to mix these three disparate terms together?

I do, I have, and hopefully, soon, you will too.

Previous overleaf: A cozy seating area provides a spot to sit in style. The black-and-white theme of this home's entry is continued to this quaint area at the base of the stairs.

Above: From this entrance hall you can see the adjoining dining room and office. Design cues such as color and pattern from the hallway were purposely introduced into each adjoining space.

Right and Opposite: If you're going to enter, then really make an entrance. Subtle in color yet dramatic in style, the wallpaper brings movement and the feeling of smoky clouds floating by as you walk through this long entry hall. The high-gloss sheen of the ceiling further elevates the space. In a long hallway such as this, it's important to treat the entire space as your foyer; thus, I duplicated the console tables with mirrors above for consistency as you walk through. There is metallic harmony in the mix of the silver mirrors with the brass console bases. I designed the clear-faceted lamp base and vases to enhance the openness. The dark oak flooring gives weight to the light color palette.

Overleaf: This family room epitomizes chic comfort. A plush sofa upholstered in durable, commercial-grade velvet contrasts nicely against the two textured side chairs. A traditional fireplace provides the focal point, while a contemporary light fixture layers gracefully overhead, creating an interesting design mix.

Previous overleaf: For the living room, formal doesn't have to translate to unusable. In this polished yet totally livable room, you'll see an inexpensive patterned rug, a custom tufted sofa, and much smaller-scale-patterned side chairs. Custom polished-nickel drapery rods perfectly fit the shape of the bay window, where the damask drapery brings in yet another pattern.

Opposite: A member of my client's family appears on this gorgeous cross-stitch art piece. The juxtaposition of the vintage art with a gilded frame against the tailored tuxedo sofa creates a match made in heaven.

Above left: Even a nondescript corner of the room can be interesting with the right art. This fascinating art piece is actually made of coconut shells.

Above right: Writing notes and even paying bills is much easier when you have this setup. My custom chair design with exposed chair spine and brass nailheads is clad in patent faux leather. The shagreen desk has texture galore that pairs like a dream with the sleek chair and patterned French-pleat drapery. The antique brass accents tie this quaint area together with the other pieces in the room.

Right: I adore a "book topper" and any type of creature, so I designed this brass octopus to creatively cap off this desktop stack of books.

"To make a room with a low ceiling look taller, hang drapery rods as close to the ceiling as possible."

Previous overleaf: This formal living room has an instant focal point with the paneled fireplace, but the wall sconces add more height and brightness. Notice how the black of the marble fireplace is extended upwards via the black of the sconce arms. The custom, blue reverse-camel-back sofa is the pièce-de-résistance of this small space. Layers of crown molding give a classic and time-honored feeling.

Opposite and above: The dining room is directly open to the hallway, so the two rooms should act as not-so-distant cousins. A tray ceiling and crystal chandelier bring instant architecture and classicism, high-lighted by the silver, metallic wallcovering on the ceiling. The area rug is a chic partner in the room and is made of durable polyester that's been factory treated with a stain repellent.

" To visually combine two adjoining and open spaces, add a backless bench between the two areas. This will allow guests to sit on either side regardless of which room everyone is congregating in. "

Opposite: With the quick removal of the wooden top of the dining table, the custom, blue felt pool table is revealed! Slightly smaller pool cues were chosen so that no surrounding walls stopped the game. This photo angle also affords a better view of our clients' art and of the subtle fade of the custom ombré rug.

Above: My clients asked for a multifunctional dining room and here is the result. The chic dining room with an origami-like light fixture, textural draperies, and an ombré blue rug can also convert to a game room with a real pool table concealed inside the dining table. The brass insets on the sides of the dining table are drawers that simultaneously house the pool cues and balls as well as dinnertime place settings.

Talk about a total redo. This once small and underused kitchen was dramatically expanded with an extra-long center island holding court. The center portion of the island was designed around the largest size of quartz slab available (to avoid seams), and the two side pieces of the island drop down in height to draw attention to the linear design of this kitchen. Speaking of lines, take note of the angled waterfall edges and inlaid wood detail on the front of the island. I opted for a zero-pendant light design for the island, allowing the coffered ceiling to shine instead. Custom walnut cabinetry with custom polished stainless-steel pulls brings a simple yet simultaneously high-styled look to this kitchen. Most importantly, there is now plenty of seating for the entire family!

Above left: A mix of open and closed storage is important in kitchen design. This custom walnut cabinetry showcases my client's favorite stemware and serving pieces.

Above right: For a dramatic accessory in your kitchen, simply bring in an oversized vase and fill with your favorite tree branches. Here, I used blooming branches from a dogwood.

Right: Think outside the jar! Here I displayed cookies and donuts under a glass cloche rather than in a traditional cookie jar to allow the pattern of the backsplash to fully show.

Opposite: I love organic elements juxtaposed against sleek finishes. The barstools feel as if they were carved from a tree and contrast well with the adjacent quartz.

"Use lighting to designate a space and to make it feel cozier."

Opposite: What's more convenient than a kitchen nook for a quick bowl of cereal? Here we created a cozy spot with a built-in banquette, loads of seating, and drawer storage below. Two white, textured (and yes, very easy to clean, with stain-protected fabric) chairs add some leggy-ness to the closed seating of the banquette. It's always nice to balance legged furniture with furniture that hugs the floor when both are in the same room. Notice that the chandelier is finished in the same polished nickel as the kitchen pendants.

Above: Opposite this home's family room is the light and bright kitchen. The entire room is an open floor plan, and in such plans, it's critical to maintain cohesion via color, pattern, and style. The kitchen meets all the needs of a busy family, but the similar colors in the tile, cabinetry, and lighting allow the kitchen and the family room to "speak" to one another. Though very elegant, the barstools are upholstered in a wipeable vinyl for those times when baby food gets a little out of control.

Opposite: This guest bedroom mixes grays and
taupes together with touches of browns and creams.
A bedroom always needs seating, and here, a flared-arm,
skirted bench handles that task perfectly.

Above: Though this bedroom is peaceful and calm with
its layers of solid colors, critical pattern was brought in
with some simple striated drapery. The bedside table is the
epitome of function and beauty with double drawers and
open shelving.

Above: The powder bath's existing vanity was retained because of its quality and its works-with-anything stained cabinet and marble top. Polished-nickel plumbing fixtures balance the sparkle of the organic, yet chic blue, wallcovering. Small-scale marble subway-tile wainscoting is equal parts timeless and lovely. An inexpensive piece of metal wall art feels right at home here, even with its much pricier counterparts.

Opposite: I adore a powder room, and this one was designed to be adored. An elegant wallcovering mural full of rich jewel tones and pattern seems to fly around the room. A complex shade of green brings the small space to life via an unexpected and fresh color choice.

Opposite: The rich stained walls and ceiling of this home office pique your interest as you see it from the home's main entry hall. Custom woodwork details give a stately backdrop to the touches of blue and white throughout the room. Care was even taken to choose recessed can trims that blend with the warm stained wood.

Above: This home office was outfitted in a caramel stained wood, which is a somewhat traditional feel for a library. However, to amp things up, faux leather ceiling inserts were installed between the coffers.

"A home theater should have some of the drama of a real movie theater, so consider what makes the movie-going experience unique and bring that home with you."

Opposite above: A wet bar was created, complete with a sink, refrigerator, and candy station. Beautiful marble and brass tile livens up this small kitchen, and the space can easily be closed off with just a pull of the drapery tassel.

Opposite left and above: Here, a gorgeous and dramatic acoustical 3D wallcovering was chosen to properly insulate the sound in this home theater. In addition, a state-of-the-art theater sound system, projector, and screen were installed for a true theatrical experience.

Front cabinetry houses some of the theater components while also providing more storage. The wood detail is continued with dark-gray-painted wall paneling throughout the rest of the room, providing the optimal background for the art-deco-inspired wall sconces. Look up and you will see wallcovering with embedded crystals that almost look like twinkling stars. Pop the popcorn and settle into the plush, oversized, custom sofa and chaise lounges. Bonus: the two front chaises can be pulled together to make one large lounging area.

Above top: Here, a formerly unused rooftop was transformed to create an entire outdoor, multifunctional living space. The floor plan was critical to this large rooftop design. It had to function as an entertaining area with options for seating, lounging, eating, meal preparation, sunbathing, and exercise. An extra-long bar was made of large-slab porcelain tile (perfect for outdoor spaces as it doesn't fade or wear) that extends all the way across the rear of the rooftop, which is anchored in the center by a gas fireplace. Glass was added to the

top of the rooftop sidewalls to create a safer environment while also blocking sometimes strong Southern California winds.

Above below: The ultimate goal of the rooftop was to capitalize on the views while making a multifunctional and chic space. The outdoor kitchen was added to allow for proper entertaining, with a sink and a refrigerator with an ice maker.

Previous overleaf: A seamless transition between the family room and the backyard was a necessity for this home. The wall of doors stack back completely inside the wall for a true indoor-outdoor experience. The large stone patio was designed as a practical and functional extension of the interior. The oversized wood and iron dining table is highlighted by five hanging pendants for perfect nighttime dining. In the distance is the roofed pergola, constructed as a semiprivate spot to relax. Meanwhile, the full outdoor kitchen provides an extra place to prepare meals.

Above: The covered pergola is a restful retreat for reading a book or just taking a nap. Pebbles were used as the base for a more natural and Zen feeling. The entire structure was built on a raised platform to add interest with varying heights to the backyard. The pergola was painted in the trim color of the home to tie the two structures together.

THE BOLD &
THE BEAUTIFUL

To be bold means different things to different people. Some might consider a colorful area rug as venturing outside of their comfort zone, while another is adventurous enough to try out a new tile design for their bathroom. To me, bold means taking calculated risks in anticipation that the reward will far surpass any angst I felt on the path to get there.

I have always considered myself a risk taker. What's the worst that could happen? I have to repaint a wall or replace a window treatment? I admit, it's a bit easier for me to say these things considering that it's my career to study and hone my design craft to the point that all design decisions aren't as risky as they might seem to you. Despite this, I invite you to also make some bold moves in your own home. Not sure where to start? Well, this chapter is the perfect muse for your bold endeavor.

This chapter showcases some of my boldest designs. This doesn't mean being bold solely with color choices, so keep your eyes open for bold patterns, materials, lighting, artwork, and furniture (and yes, admittedly some bold color too). I like to make one bold move in my life each day, and this practice has sharpened my boldness to where it's no longer such a scary task for me to think along audacious lines. If you're timid, start small: change your shower curtain, paint an accent wall (yes, I'm a designer that still stands behind a well-planned accent wall), or buy some funky-patterned toss pillows. Soon, you will sharpen your own boldness skills and be ready to tackle large-scale bold projects.

Page 86: This open-plan dining room needed to grab your attention as soon as you walked into the front door, and I say mission accomplished! The design plan started with the unique blue, silver, and black flame-stitch-style striped wallcovering, and the rest is history. Remember what I said about a starting point for your design? Well, this was mine. The rug works because of the larger-scaled pattern, and the blue leather side chairs and velvet head chairs pull the wallpaper colors down to eye level. A custom brass and walnut dining table further plays off the linear lines throughout. The star attraction could very well be the starburst brass and glass light fixture.

Above: Looking back to the entry of this home, a linear glass and wood front door design opens into the hallway leading to the rest of the home. Look closely in the wainscoting and you'll see one of my favorite tricks: hidden closet storage behind wainscoting.

Opposite: Swivel chairs are a great way to create a seating area. Here, four chairs are upholstered in a soft and supple bouclé fabric. The coffee and side tables are in natural, organic shapes to pay homage to the mountains outside.

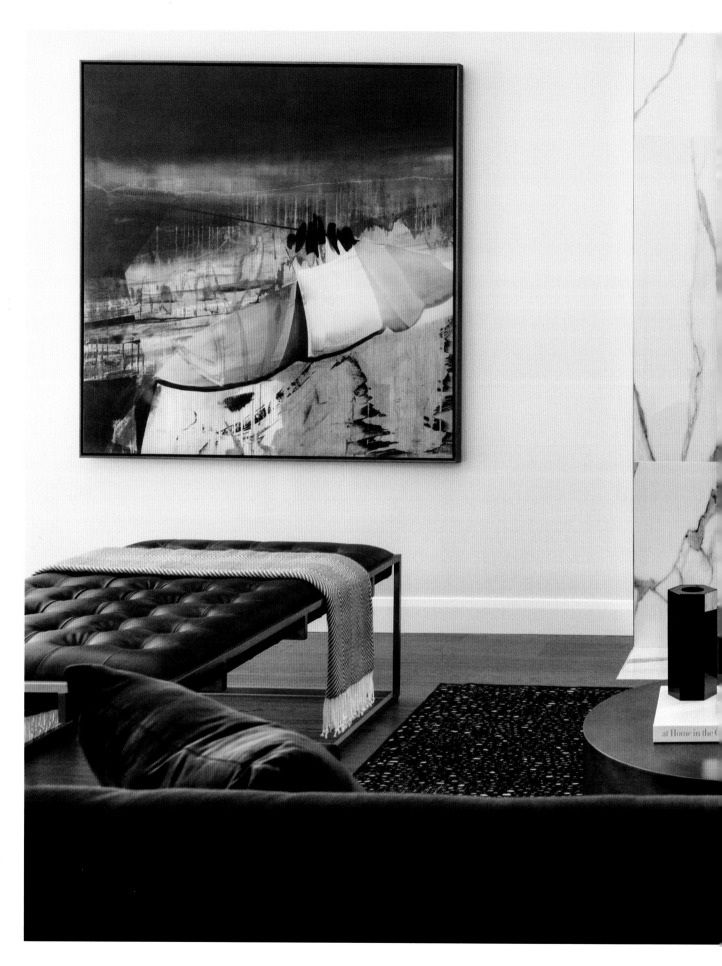

Previous overleaf: The fireplace is the center of the entire living and dining area in this family home. Large-scale porcelain tile mimics the look of real marble without compromising ease of maintenance. Circular coffee tables in varying heights can be accessed from the sofa or the bench. Punchy, bold art by Sarah Stockstill adds an almost art gallery feel to the room.

Opposite: In an open floor plan, it's critical that you caringly scatter the color from one area to the next. Here, the rich cobalt blue of the swivel chair is instantly relatable to the wallcovering in the adjacent office. Art by Jean Kenna wakes up a neutral wall while also tying in the colors in the entire open space.

This page: Being bold also means bold accessory choices that blend well with a room's furnishings. Notice the play on lines in the chair, side table, and even the gold vase.

" The key to keeping
consistency through-
out an open floor
plan is the 'sprin-
kling' of the same
materials and colors
throughout each
adjoining space. "

Opposite: I knew the fireplace needed to be the focal point of this family room for a couple of reasons. First, there was a need for pattern and height on this side of the room to balance the high kitchen cabinets on the opposite side. Second, with all of the neutral walls and cabinetry, a bold pattern was required to wake this wall up. Though it looks like one large slab of marble, this is actually composed of large cut pieces of marble carefully laid out to resemble the pattern of one big, solid piece. TIP: If you are hanging a television above a fireplace, you must consider the heat of the fireplace. The TV was recessed into the fireplace wall, and a mantel was added to deflect heat.

Above: This kitchen and family room could easily be one of my top favorite designs. Continuing the bold and beautiful theme, we carried the blues into these spaces with paint, art, and the area rug. Of course, there are more brass accents, which lend an elegance to each room; these details span even down to the color of the toss pillows. The custom, gray modular sectional is upholstered in my signature commercial-grade velvet but this time with some subtle pattern. A room fit for a king . . . or an adorable pup!

Above: The family room is ready for . . . well, the family! A modular sofa is upholstered in washable (and removable!) covers. The round, bronze table is ready for family game night in the comfy, quilted, green-and-brass chairs. A large sculptural floor lamp brings overhead lighting without blocking the television. This room is all about comfort and ease.

Opposite: A wet bar was built in the family room. The style of the cabinetry matches that in the kitchen, but this time in a dark and rich brown. The real star of this bar is the iridescent 3D backsplash.

" When there is no room for a side table but you still need lighting, floor lamps are amazingly functional and beautiful. They also aid in creating varying heights in a room. "

THE HIGH AND LOW
OF IT ALL

One reason that design seems out of reach for so many is the price point. The observer might look at a final image of a professionally photographed space and think to themselves that they could never have or afford the things shown in that image. The reality is quite a bit different. Even in my firm's luxury, larger-budget projects, we always institute a high/low philosophy. What is high/low? It simply means choosing products at higher price points for those items that really matter the most, and at lower price points for things that do not necessarily require a higher price tag to demonstrate beauty and quality.

Some examples in my high category are sofas, coffee tables, dining chairs, beds, appliances, case goods such as nightstands and dressers, and some ceiling or wall lighting.

Examples in my low category include lamps, accessories, pillows, mirrors, and sometimes art. Essentially, think of it this way: you don't want to compromise on quality for a sofa that you are going to sit on probably every single day. But why not purchase an equally beautiful mirror that happens to cost much less than the higher priced mirror while still achieving the same look and functionality? Rest easy knowing that you saved so much money on the "low" that it allowed you to properly invest in the "high."

Previous overleaf: This entry is a feast for the eyes. I utilized my love of brass, making it the accent metal throughout all the home's spaces. Look back into the kitchen and you will see how the brass accents visually combine all the rooms. This space is bold for a few reasons: columns instead of dining room walls, wooden wall-trim details instead of simple painted drywall, and a bold blue as a color snap.

Opposite: This living room is truly a multifunctional space. The former design had multiple sunken living areas. The floor was raised to all one level, bridging the gap between all the areas. In the distance is the dining room with its punch of bold color.

Opposite and above: Custom, emerald-green wallcovering and a linear oversized pendant were designed to designate the dining area. The green accent color makes an appearance all throughout this family home.

Opposite: Small spaces need not have small design plans. This dining room is featuring its best asset, high ceilings, by drawing the eye up with large, attention-garnering pendants. The goal was to meld the upstairs sleeping loft with the downstairs, using the pendants as the conduit.

Below: The view from the sleeping loft to the dining room shows the mix of circles and squares living in perfect harmony.

Right: Creating vignettes within a vignette keeps design fun and interesting. The mix of brass, wood, black, and white is a classic, no-fail combination.

" To visually join two open spaces, add pendant lighting that spans the vertical length of both areas. "

Opposite: In this colorfully bold kitchen, a rich blue paint color coated the existing cabinetry. Some new hardware and voila: an old golden oak stained kitchen now feels current and fresh.

Above left: Elongated subway tile is a fresh design approach to the traditional smaller subway tiles.

Above right: My client requested a dedicated spot for her morning caffeine, so a coffee station was created with full storage above and below the coveted machine.

Right: Plumbing fixtures are the ideal way to add some sparkle to a kitchen. This industrial-style faucet is black and antique brass to match the pulls and knobs on the cabinetry.

Above: In one of my boldest moves, I designed this glass-front upper cabinetry to have open backs. I adore this handmade metallic tile so much that I didn't want to hide it! Thick glass shelving allows the interior lights to shine from top to bottom.

Right: This kitchen was designed with two smaller kitchen islands rather than one large one. The traffic paths through the space worked much better with separation between the two island work zones. The sink island has bar stools to pull up for a quick bite, while the center, blue island is larger and used primarily for meal prep. Drawers and storage were built into every available spot, allowing all kitchenware to be out of sight. Marble-look quartz countertops are both beautiful and functional. An oval, iron-and-rough-hewn-wood table along with leather director chairs bring in an organic touch to the breakfast nook and pair well to the bar stools.

Above: The kitchen was completely gutted and redesigned in an updated traditional style. Greige cabinets in an adapted Shaker style feel right at home here. Textured subway tile and a cabinetry-wrapped vent hood only add to the classic feel. Notice how the dark refrigerator-wall cabinetry brings in some contrast. The flooring features a herringbone inset edged in brass trim.

Opposite: Doing dishes isn't so bad with this setup. Modern wall sconces juxtapose perfectly against the traditional tile. The woven black shades allow for light filtering but are transparent enough to still show the view.

"Window treatments need not be fussy to be effective. Consider using wooden shades in lieu of fabric for a clean and functional result. "

" When painting a room
a dark color, be sure you
have adequate natural
and artificial lighting. "

Opposite: I love a stately and attention-commanding office, and this one is both of those things. Dark-gray, industrial metal furniture; a rich, deep shade of paint on the wall; and subtly patterned drapery are all interesting but monochromatic so that they don't get in the way of a productive workday.

Above: This office was created by building a wall to separate it from the living room. Two pocket doors painted in my favorite shade of black (aptly named Caviar) can be closed for more privacy.

Left: A nontraditional bookcase design adds architecture to the room while also providing the perfect spot for books and family mementos.

Above: A swing seat was installed into the custom, geometric ceiling design in the sitting area of this young girl's room. An essential desk is ideal for homework or crafts, while a sofa bed says it's time for a sleepover! I love using a shag rug in kids' rooms, as I know they will be nestled into it at some point.

Opposite: Two separate bedrooms were combined to form this large room for a teenager. It's light, airy, and full of fun!

Above: This main bedroom has its own entryway, so I lowered the ceiling in the entry while raising the ceiling in the bedroom. The abrupt transition to a full-height room makes the room feel even higher. This technique was often used by Frank Lloyd Wright in his designs.

Right: I designed this Brutalist-style console as an artistic play on shadows. The touch-latch doors open to provide extra storage.

Opposite: A custom, diamond-tufted headboard stands guard at command central in the main bedroom. Notice the oversized width of the footboard: big enough to sit for a second or even to hold your iPad or laptop. The pattern of the burl nightstands gives a nice contrast and color to the otherwise neutral palette.

Overleaf: The irregular layout of this main bedroom didn't prevent a beautiful design. The four-post bed was centered in the room under the cluster-pendant light fixture. The windows are not at the same level; this was disguised by installing the shades and drapery at the same height for the illusion of equal windows. This rug is completely machine washable, in case of little pet accidents.

" Use appropriately sized
mirrors and lamps to
balance the height of beds
with tall headboards. "

WHAT LIES BENEATH

Color is also a critical part to effectively mixing design elements and styles. Look at the undertones of the colors that interest you. By undertone, I am referring to the very basis or background of the predominant color. Black and brown are always my favorite undertones to blend into my designs, but this philosophy can work with any color. For instance, if you have a gray wallcovering, train your eye to see what the basis of that gray color is. Is it black? Brown? Blue? Trust me, there is a visible undertone present, and you must find it in order to perfectly blend the various pieces in your room.

Here's an exercise: visit your local home improvement store, or pull out a paint deck if you have one, and find a color you like that is also on a paint card with other colors in lighter and darker shades or tones. As you review the card or paint deck, look at the color at the very bottom or top of that paint card and you will see the genesis of all of the colors in between.

Once you determine this all-important color undertone, make sure the main design components of your room also have this same undertone in them.

"Nightstands are better used when there are various shelves and drawers. Clutter can be hidden below, and the top can stay neat and tidy."

Above: The guest room is a departure from the bold color seen elsewhere in this home. A tone-on-tone wallpaper brings a great backdrop to the walnut headboard, while two cylindrical brass tables are a unique departure from the traditional nightstand.

Opposite: Blue, textured nightstands with brass accents are extending the color continuity from downstairs to the sleeping loft of this condo. Simple, curvaceous lamps are whimsical and beautifully feminine.

RYAN KORBAN

JAY JEFFERS | BE BOLD

Above: A formerly cramped and awkwardly laid out main bath was redesigned for modern-day use. A soaking tub found a home beside the large shower and alongside a custom, dark-brown double-sink vanity. The floor tile was installed with a contrasting band to create the feel of an area rug.

Left: Of course, the green theme of the home is added to the main bathroom, with a crushed velvet ottoman that can tuck neatly under the makeup vanity just across from the sink vanity.

Opposite: I showed you one of my favorite kitchen designs, so now I'll show you one of my favorite powder room designs. This bold tile was inspired by a subway tile I saw literally in the London subway. The handmade, forest-green tile has hints of black and gray and irregular edges that bring a real sense of relaxed beauty to this space. I chose a herringbone installation pattern for even more visual interest. The other three walls are clad in a gold, metallic wallcovering. Again, organic touches instantly relax a room, so the natural marble countertop is a nice contrast to the brass base of the vanity.

Opposite: This small bathroom needed cohesiveness, so the marble-look porcelain tile is carried from the floor, up both end walls behind the vanity, and into the shower (as seen in the reflection of the mirror).

Above left: Honeycomb marble tile clads all the walls in this bath. I have an affinity for using wall tiles floor-to-ceiling to create an effect similar to wallpaper.

Above right: The upstairs bathroom in this condo is a mix of old and new. I kept the original tub and white subway tile but awakened it with a linear, hexagonal-shaped floor tile. A black vanity with marble countertop mixes black and brass accents via plumbing fixtures, pulls, and light fixtures. Don't be afraid to mix your metals!

Right: All white bathrooms need not be boring! Here, a stripe was added with a deep blue subway tile that carries the eye completely around the space.

Opposite: This guest bath needed to have ease of use and cleanup, and the curbless shower is ideal for a person of any age to walk right in. The floor tile is continued up the walls of the shower in the same stacked pattern. A teak bench adds organic practicality.

Above: Laundry rooms should be beautiful too! Here, I carried the timeless blue from the rest of the house into the laundry room.

Everything has its place here, including a drying station, a hidden kitty litter box, and plenty of storage. The entire room is finished with tile on floors and walls, so function is not lost for aesthetics. The open walnut shelving is both useful and a nice contrast to the painted finishes in the room. Even the bold area rug is made of vinyl for worry-free laundry time.

Above: A classic design for a home theater. Ruby-red velvet lines the walls, which also showcase custom woodwork details. The sofa gives space to spread out, while the theater chairs can recline and are complete with cup holders.

Opposite: The front area of the theater resembles the theaters of yesteryear, with fringed drapery surrounding the screen. The cabinetry on both sides of the screen house all of the media components for the theater and the entire home. Door pulls were left off so the doors looked more like built-in wall details.

NEUTRAL TERRITORY

I think neutrals get a bad rap. Some people see them as simplistic and boring or as an easy way out of making design decisions. If done correctly, neutrals can be exciting, interesting, and even challenging to assemble. I remember when I was a new designer on HGTV, the homeowner specifically requested all light-hued neutrals in her home. I set out on a mission to expand her horizons and convert her and her husband to a more colorful palette. Being a new designer at the time, I felt color was the design element that really stood out on television, and I was determined to make this couple see the power of it while simultaneously making my room design a memorable one. As the process went along, however, I began to understand why neutrals were so important to some people and to design in general.

Neutrals are cleansing to the eye. They give us a serene and simple background on which to layer other design elements. Neutrals do not only mean white walls and light-toned floors, but neutrals also take on many forms. Consider the color white—most people don't realize that white paint has so many iterations. Do you prefer warm or cool? Do you like a gray undertone or perhaps a pink or blue one? If done correctly, neutrals can add a lot of depth to any design.

Back to that family on HGTV that I was hell-bent on changing. Not only was the wife not open to moving away from her beloved neutrals (if you look up the episode you will see her term is "milky"), but she forced me to quickly realize that *clients* live in the homes I am designing, *not me*. I then revamped my entire design plan for those TV clients to focus on making neutrals something that we could all believe in. The result: a bedroom that had a neutral backdrop layered with patina-covered antiques, textured rugs, accessories, pillows, and even hints of color brought in through easily removable accessories and accents. The big reveal showed that I had done my job right, with hugs all around. The lesson is this: neutrals are not anti-design. In fact, they can be more complicated than creating a color-filled room. In this chapter, I am going to show you some of my favorite projects filled with light and airy neutral color palettes and reveal to you why they work. Namaste. You're in neutral territory now.

Previous overleaf: This sinuous, curved staircase is the first thing you see as you enter this sophisticated farmhouse. The simplicity and beauty of the staircase design was meant to be reminiscent of the flowing river just outside. Stair treads were salvaged from a historic home that was being torn down.

Above: This home received a major makeover, starting at the front door! The entire entry was lowered in height to match the rest of the home, affording the opportunity to install a much-taller front door. My love of linear is evident in this room.

Opposite: Fireplace details and a coffee table with flowers, books, and a metallic piece—my no-fail way to dress a coffee table.

GUCCI THE MAKING OF

THE BIG BOOK OF THE HAMPTONS

AMERICAN FASHION

THE GREAT AMERICAN HOUSE   Gil Schafer III

"Using varying shades or hues of a color or finish is part of the professional designer's bag of tricks for giving a room depth of color."

The family room is centered by the floor-to-ceiling fireplace, which is clad in metallic tile. Custom, square-armed Chesterfield sofas form a traditional furniture plan layout with matching console tables and lamps. The patterned rug gives movement to the room, while my client's favorite art by photographer Joel Sartore reminds him of the scenery just outside his front door.

" Harness the power of interior and under-cabinet lighting. This simple addition can illuminate your cabinetry in the most subtle and lovely ways. I opt for remote-controlled LED tape lighting in most instances. "

Previous overleaf: Post-renovation, the family room is open to the kitchen, and the design scheme extends to this side of the room. A comfy, textured velvet sectional is the ideal spot to cozy up in front of the stacked-stone marble fireplace.

Left and above: The key to good shelf appeal is mixing books with accessories. On these shelves, there are a plethora of books, organic and metallic objects, and photos.

Previous overleaf: This dining room is anchored by the elongated live-edge table. Attention to detail was very important in this room, with neutral chairs sitting on a patterned-hide area rug. Silk draperies bring sparkle and elegance. The home was built on a former horse farm, and the mirror has the look of a horse bridle to honor the home's past.

Above: A small section of wall is awakened with one of my favorite design pieces: a bar cart! There is something about the beauty of mobile liquor that makes me smile. On a more serious note, the bronze bar cart is further highlighted by the metal-clad wooden sculpture. Family photos give depth to the space when hung in the adjacent hallway.

Opposite: The dining room is directly adjacent to the kitchen on the following page, and blue chairs extend the color to this side of the space. The shadow-casting pendant is made of a type of rattan called buri ting ting. The wall art is from the homeowners' vintage racing poster collection.

Previous overleaf: This kitchen went from supporting actor to the true scene stealer! A massive structural beam was added to allow multiple formerly compartmentalized rooms to be combined into one large kitchen. Gray, custom cabinetry and quartz counters are the ideal start for this neutral palette.

Opposite: What do you do when you have too much space in a kitchen?! Create a bar area, of course! Notice the repeat of the open wood shelving from the opposite side of the room to create balance.

Above left: Elongated subway tiles give the perfect neutral background on which to layer this kitchen's full design plan.

Above right: Cocktails always have my name on them.

Right: This kitchen has some unique features. Polished stainless-steel tubing with matte black connector joints provides chic support for the island extension. The hexagonal blue tile pays homage to the ocean breeze that can be felt in this home. All of the elements combine to form a perfect design trifecta of materials.

Previous overleaf: The kitchen is the true heart of this home. A supremely large island showcases book-matched marble slabs and is big enough to seat six people comfortably. Bronze metal bar stools with leather seats add some elegance.

Opposite: The red accents from the range knobs and pots and pans demonstrate how small touches of color will allow their neutral counterparts to shine even more.

Above: The handmade glazed metallic, subway tile deepens the neutral palette, and reclaimed wooden shelves rest on black support arms.

Opposite: The sinuous curves of the staircase lead to this uniquely curved landing. A small nook is the perfect spot to add a writing desk and chair.

Above: A home office was designed with built-in cabinetry for a work desk and plenteous storage. The backs of the bookcases are lined with metallic wallpaper.

Previous overleaf: The main bedroom extends the neutral
palette of this home upstairs with a gray, tweed headboard and
a gray bench mixed with shades of gray on the walls, bedding,
and window treatments. Why it works: the eye sees the same
color displayed with varying textures, which makes this space
interesting.

Above: Silk drapery is made couture when outlined with
patterned trim. The bubbled mercury-glass lamp base provides
a bit of glam in this room.

Opposite: This guest room bed was designed to tuck the mirror
perfectly into the headboard's inset. Window treatments with
circular patterns tie into the shape of the headboard. Leather-
wrapped nightstands are outlined with nickel nailhead trim.

" Carrara marble
(or Carrara-marble-
look tile) is an easy
match to almost
any wall color or
wall tile. "

The main bathroom was carved out of a former closet and
a much smaller bathroom and is now one big space with
room for a freestanding tub, a black-stained double vanity,
and a separate shower. The sloped ceiling design was part
necessity and part intention: the exterior wall required the
slope, and it was matched on the interior wall to create a
unique and cozy feeling.

Above and right: The double sink vanities are white, Shaker-style cabinets. Above them, the mirror-framed mirrors are outlined in brass to tie in the tub pendant. Marble floors are heated for warmth in the winter. The home's soft wall-paint color is seen throughout the main bedroom suite.

Opposite: Sometimes the simplest component can create an intriguing design. Behind this freestanding tub, I installed a wall of wood that was salvaged from an old barn. The mineral-stained poplar species of wood was sanded and sealed (no stain added) and simply applied to the wall behind and above the tub to create a truly unique canopy. Bonus points if you spot the dolphin that appeared in the wood grain.

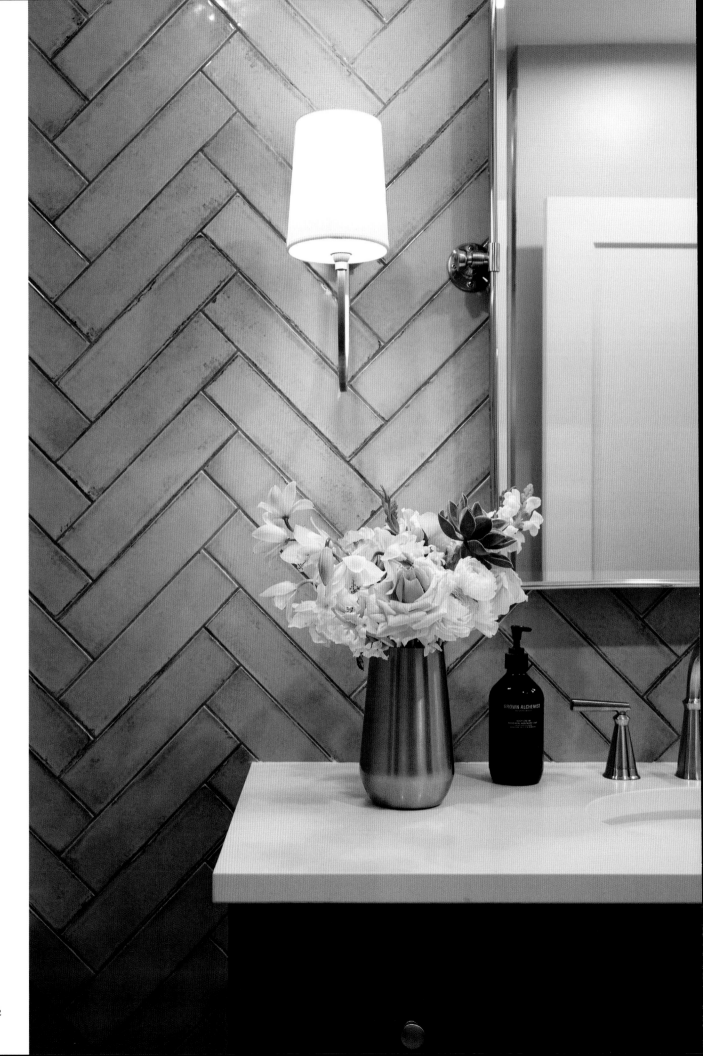

Opposite: The upstairs hall bath is a decidedly softer palette. Pale blue-gray tiles with irregular, darker edges are installed in a herringbone pattern. Satin-nickel lights and plumbing fixtures do not compete for attention with anything else in the room, resulting in a uniform feel.

Above right: This downstairs hall bath packs a punch in the form of patterns in shades of black. Matte black plumbing fixtures and black-and-brass light fixtures add some "design jewelry" to the room and coordinate nicely with the brass pulls on the charcoal-gray vanity.

Right: Penny tiles give grip and good design to the shower floor. See how these tiles are layered on top of the geometric lines of the bathroom floor and contrast in pattern with the white subway tile with black grout. A linear drain adds modernity to a very industrial feel.

Page 164: This client's energetic art by Hal Larsen livens up the custom-built, floating, walnut cabinetry. The midcentury-inspired chair and side table have the clean lines needed to juxtapose the artwork.

Previous overleaf: This living room renovation of a midcentury home resulted in a mix of warm woods and sleek metals with lots of color accents. The custom stainless-steel-clad fireplace is the focal point of the open space and is purposely visible from almost every adjoining room.

Opposite: The view from the entry into the formal living room showcases the home's original 1920s baluster—one of the few remaining original pieces salvaged after an earthquake damaged the home years ago. Notice how the hand-planed beams in the formal living room carry the sultry darkness of the flooring into that space.

Above: The front door was custom stained to match the flooring. Placement of the windows was key in bringing in natural light as well a fresh, asymmetrical feeling. A shagreen console provides both storage and beauty at the entry.

Right: The mantra for the update for this 1920s home was "movement." The grand entry was completely overhauled, beginning with dark stained floors, contemporary wallcovering, colorful stair runner, and culminating with a grand ceiling design reminiscent of the vaulted ceiling on Ellis Island in New York City.

> "When accessorizing your shelves for that perfect "shelfie," it's important to mix sizes, shapes, colors, and finishes. I consider shelves a microcosm of the room they are in."

Opposite: In a neutral room, it's important to have something that brings impact. A rich blue sofa grabs your attention, and if that's not enough, the sexy and colorful art by Elena Carlie demands more than a glance.

Above: Mixing your favorite older pieces alongside new ones is a great way to accessorize bookshelves. Here, pieces from Asian travels blend well with a bold, modern vase.

" Flowers and plants
are valuable design
elements that
bring instant vital-
ity and color into
a room. "

This pied-à-terre is small in size but huge in character. The 1960s, midcentury condo was originally designed by famed architect Ray Kappe. Here in the living room, the floor-to-ceiling windows were retained but softened by silvery gray sheers.

"If you don't have a traditional coffee table, cluster several smaller tables together to create the effect of one larger center table."

Opposite: The living room is a lesson in symmetry and shape. Two black ceruse-treated bookcases flank the prismatic walnut credenza. The brass on each piece ties them together.

Above: The toss pillows are fun and colorful—evocative of what could have been used in this home in the past.

Opposite: The den retained the base of the original walnut cabinetry but was revised with floating shelves above. A custom sectional with a built-in console and side table is midcentury style though updated with deeper, plusher seating. A multilevel, round coffee table is important to contrast with all the linear aspects of the den.

Above: The lake view of this home is integral to the design, both inside and out. Finishes were chosen to accentuate the view.

"Statement walls
are a great design
feature to easily
create a focal point
in a specific space."

The midcentury-inspired wall mural is new, while the small table and chairs belonged to the previous owners—who happen to be the new owner's parents. Unique standing metal art finds its home on the stair ledge.

Above: The view from the living area to the kitchen shows how the spaces relate to each other. Tonalities in color blend the room with ease. Here is also a great view of the atom-like glass light fixture, which proves that organic design elements do not always have to be made of materials actually found in nature.

Opposite: The kitchen was fully updated, including covering an unnecessary window to create more usable space. The square wall tile extends from countertop to ceiling and reflects the views of the Hollywood Hills outside. A round, midcentury-style table is right at home, while clear acrylic chairs were used in this small space to prevent it from feeling over crowded.

Opposite: The kitchen was designed as a blend of metallics with a touch of color. This mix is well balanced with the silvery etching on the marble backsplash, stainless-steel appliances, antique brass highlights on the cabinetry, and a rich blue island. Black countertops are timeless and elegant.

Above: The adjacent butler's pantry is neatly tucked away between the kitchen and dining room. Butler's pantries are great for creating storage and much-needed work zones. Here we have glass cabinetry with metallic wallpaper to add some sparkle to the back.

Overleaf: Not all spaces were totally redone in this historic home, and the kitchen is one of them. The Shaker cabinetry was updated with inlaid brass trim and painted a creamy white. The backsplash continues the movement mantra of this home's entry with laser-cut silver-and-white marble. An arch added at the kitchen entry references the home's front door.

Above: This bedroom faces a beautiful lake, and two midcentury-style chairs furnish a reading spot like no other.

Opposite: The main bedroom feels as if it was almost carved out to create this cozy and modern bed nook. Metallic cork wallcovering adds contemporary texture, while the wooden bed and nightstands bring in the nature that midcentury design embraces.

Opposite: Glamour and midcentury beauty meet for a fun time in the bedroom. A black accent wall and a plush area rug contrast nicely with the brass accents on the nightstands, light, and poufs.

Above: The silhouette of the table lamp further enhances the midcentury feel.

Opposite above: The dramatic motorized drapery in this bedroom not only acts as a wall-to-wall design element, but the sound dampening effects are tremendous. I knew we needed a burl chest and a mirror on this wall, but how to achieve that with the drapery? The solution was to attach the mirror to a wall arm that slips between two drapery panels; and the result is a mirror that seems to magically float on its own.

Opposite below: The main bedroom also has a cozy seating nook with a custom brown velvet sectional supported on brass feet. The two ottomans provide extra storage. The extra-plush area rug was simply cut from a large roll of carpet. Artwork is personal to any home, and in particular, this artwork by James Coates means the world to these clients.

Above: This client loves red, so we brought it front and center in the main bedroom. A drapery pocket with hidden LED lighting was added to the ceiling so the detailed drapery and pleated sheers tuck away perfectly. The oak and brass four-poster bed accentuates the high ceilings. Beautiful wall sconces provide lovely task lighting; and not seen are reading lights that tuck away behind the headboard when not in use.

Above: Custom wallpaper in the powder room uses ancient letters and symbols to spell out words such as *joy*, *hope*, and *bliss*. The contemporary vanity and a brass mirror of my own design contrast nicely with one another.

Opposite above: Complete with metallic porcelain tile wainscoting and energetic green animal print wallpaper, this is one punchy powder room! The sink and faucets were existing in the home, but worked so well that I decided to keep them in the new design.

Above: The makeup vanity for this main bath was built at counter height and uses an adjustable stool. This consistency in height makes for a much cleaner look than a traditional sink/makeup vanity with varying heights.

Opposite: Admittedly, the main bathroom purposely leans more toward the modern side of midcentury, but the magic of the tile movement on the walls and floors recalls the lake just outside. The square lines of the tub are replicated in the rectangular sinks and cabinetry hardware.

THE
HOLLYWOOD
EFFECT

The glitz and glamour of old (and new) Hollywood have long held a special place in my heart. I can't take my eyes off of the shine and sparkle of an actress's gown as she saunters down the red carpet. I feel a maximalist, sexy, and complex range of emotions when I see Hollywood style done right—in both fashion and home design. In Hollywood, a mirrored chandelier is much more exciting than a painted one, and an area rug will usually have a detailed pattern rather than only a solid color.

The magic potion for designing with the Hollywood effect is to thoroughly think through all of the design elements and how they interact with each other. While this is important in any design plan, it is particularly important when selecting materials for a glamorous design. Hollywood glam can go from just enough to very wrong with just one bad choice. It's important to know that while a little goes a long way, too little can seem deflated and lacking.

I'm going to show you how to bring the glamour of old and new Hollywood into your home. You'll see evidence of it in fabrics, rugs, lighting, and accessories, but I also want you to take note of how these glamorous rooms are balanced with neutrals, which keep the home from looking garish or overdone.

Grab your ticket, dahhling; you have a front row seat for my personal tour of glamorous home design!

> " If the perfect extra-large coffee table can't be found, place two coffee tables together to form one larger table. "

Page 196: The view into this glamour-filled dining room showcases the detail in the drapery trim and the coordination of the subdued color palette. Brass accents on the mirror, chairs, and sideboard hold hands with the mirrored chandelier. It was important to also add the dark stained wood of the table and side chairs for proper contrast.

Page 198: Again, my bar cart obsession finds its way into this home. The sleek modern design of this gold one is already a Hollywood classic. Mixing gold tones into the silver tones of this home is the perfect choice to add warmth and interest to a cool palette.

Page 199: The curved design of the head chair brings interest and variation when placed against the simple rectilinear lines of the wainscoting. The oversized mirror draws the eye up toward the ceiling molding detail while reflecting a chandelier that would make any Hollywood star jealous.

Previous Overleaf: An art-deco-inspired black sofa is the spot to be in the formal living room. Brass accents continue throughout the home with the soft curves of the table legs, chairs, and side tables. In the distance, catch a peek of the oversized starburst chandelier in the entry.

Opposite: A curvaceous, marble fireplace takes center stage in the midst of custom bookcases. It's important to coordinate elements such as the fireplace and bookcases, and here we use the curves of each to join them together.

Above: I prefer a mix of seating types in a living room. Here a comfy and practical swivel chair can be turned toward the conversational area of the sectional or toward the lake view out the windows.

"Don't underestimate the power of trim on furniture or drapery to make something ho-hum turn totally honorable. Trim comes in lots of options, from fringe to cording or even fabric tape."

This angle of the formal living room shows the floor-to-ceiling drapery, which frames the view of the pool and the peaceful lake outside. The gold starburst console cabinet pairs well with the starburst light fixture in the entry.

Previous overleaf: This bathroom is a true play on pattern, with varying sizes of marble from the oversized floor, rectangular-sized wainscoting, and mirrored, patterned upper wall tiles. Symmetry was created with a freestanding tub flanked by two custom stained wood vanities. I designed the vanity countertops with extra height for added drama.

Opposite: I realize I have said this before, but this is truly one of my favorite powder-room designs. The grass-cloth wallpaper has embroidered beads to create subtle stripes. The tile design takes a simple-shaped tile and arranges it in a fresh new way. Brass accents complete this dark and sexy space.

Above left: The makeup vanity was tucked into a niche between the toilet room and closet. Polished-nickel cup pulls add some sparkle. For more glam, the decorative mirror is mounted onto a full-wall mirror.

Above right: Unapologetic glamour coming right up! A custom, stained-glass door opens onto this lavish bathroom. The soft curves of the freestanding tub invite you to relax and look up at the crystal chandelier above your head. Mirrored tile inside the tub niche sparkles and shines when the hidden lights begin to reflect.

Right: This bathroom was a total renovation. Heated marble floors form a luxe floor, and floating vanities with LED, under-cabinet lighting are even more accentuated with the heavily patterned, blue granite countertops. The curbless shower is steam, chromatherapy, and aromatherapy and has lots of spray options to bathe in high style.

EPILOGUE

I sincerely hope this book has ignited the flame of the designer within you! While truly great interior design can be a daunting endeavor, there are many ways to change the home you live in with minimal effort. My real purpose is to start a conversation, one that will be a fruitful discussion inside your own household to spark change with the things you can do. I like to say that interior design changes lives, and I truly believe if you follow the tips and instructions laid out in this book, you will not only change your environment and your life but you'll even have fun doing it! Each day is filled with new opportunities to improve the world we live in. Why not use those precious moments to find ways to enrich your own life and the lives of those around you?

Start at home. I promise it will be worth the effort.

Thank you for reading!
John

ACKNOWLEDGMENTS

Creating this book has been the culmination of a lifetime of dreaming and planning. As my inspiration in life and business Dolly Parton says in her lyrics for *Try*, all dreams need wings to truly make them fly. I would like to introduce you to the people who are my wings.

Thank you to the entire team at Gibbs Smith for supporting my dream of this book, and particularly to Madge Baird, for wisely and patiently guiding me throughout the entire process. Thanks also to Rita Sowins for a beautiful book design.

To my husband, Peter, thank you for constantly believing in me and encouraging me to always follow my heart. This book, and so many other amazing things in life, are because of you. I'll always blow a kiss your way; I love you infinitely.

To my parents and grandparents, thank you for always allowing me to follow my passion, no matter what society said was the practical path to take.

To my mother, Sherry, especially, your talents, creativity, and wanderlust are a big piece of my life and success today. Thank you for introducing me to the beautiful, sacred space of "home."

Huge thanks to my valued clients for placing your trust in me with something as sacred as your home. The journey is truly as exciting as the destination.

Loren Ruch, from the very moment we met, I felt your friendship and support. I'm always ready for a pina colada with you.

Michele Bolen, that first opportunity to showcase my design chops on national television, spurred my design career as I know it today. I am so grateful.

Heather Rau, my Senior Designer and mind reader, your talents are far more numerous than you even realize. The projects in this book are also a result of your hard work and immense skills, and I am humbly grateful.

My entire John McClain Design team, your ability to fulfill my vision never fails to impress me. Thank you for your loyalty and hard work.

Neal Wagner and Thomas Piscitello, you both gave me a crash course in design and big-picture thinking. Thank you for imparting your fabulous knowledge to me.

Jess Ponce, thank you for your ability to relay so effortlessly what I am thinking. Your understanding of my vision is the very reason for *The Designer Within*.

To Cindy Bertram, your keen writing skills never cease to amaze me. Thank you for making my sometimes manic thoughts translate to paper. Most importantly, thank you for being a friend.

Thank you to all of the fabulously talented photographers whose work is seen in this book: Zeke Ruelas, Stephen Allen, Michael Scott, Lauren Pressey, and Larry Taylor. My projects are only as good as they are shown, and you make them (and me) truly shine.

First Edition
26 25 24 23 22   5 4 3 2 1

Text © 2022 John McClain
Photographic credits:

© 2022 Zeke Ruelas:
Back cover, 2–3, 4, 8, 11, 13, 18, 20–85, 92–93, 104–107, 113, 121, 125 top right, 132, 136–139, 143–147, 153–155, 158–159, 162–163, 168–175, 180–185, 188–193

© 2022 Stephen Allen:
1, 86, 94–95, 98–99, 108–109, 112, 116–117, 120, 123, 124, 235 bottom right, 126–127, 128 left, 130, 133–135, 140–142, 148–149, 151, 152, 156-157, 160–161, 198, 206–209, 212–213, 216–217, 221

© 2022 Michael Scott:
Cover, 164, 166–167, 176–179, 186–187, 194–196, 199, 200–202, 204–205, 210–211, 214–215, 218–219, 220

© 2022 Lauren Pressey:
6, 88–89, 90–91, 96, 97, 100, 102–103, 110–111, 114–115, 118, 122, 125 top left

© 2022 Larry Taylor:
128–129 right, 150

© 2022 Amy Lamb:
Author portrait on jacket flap

Published by
Gibbs Smith
P.O. Box 667
Layton, Utah 84041

1.800.835.4993 orders
www.gibbs-smith.com

Designed by Rita Sowins / Sowins Design
Printed and bound in China

Gibbs Smith books are printed on either recycled, 100% post-consumer waste, FSC-certified papers or on paper produced from sustainable PEFC-certified forest/controlled wood source. Learn more at www.pefc.org.

Library of Congress Control Number: 2022930967
ISBN: 978-1423660224